RAINFOREST
BIRDS

Text and photography by Edward Parker

an imprint of Hodder Children's Books

© 2002 White-Thomson Publishing Ltd

Produced for Hodder Wayland by
White-Thomson Publishing Ltd
2/3 St. Andrew's Place
Lewes, East Sussex
BN7 1UP

Editor: Sarah Doughty
Design: Bernard Higton
Text consultant: Dr Paul Toyne

Published in Great Britain in 2002 by Hodder Wayland,
an imprint of Hodder Children's Books.
This paperback edition published in 2003.
Reprinted in 2004.

Produced in association with WWF–UK.
WWF–UK registered charity number 1081247.
A company limited by guarantee number 4016725.
Panda device © 1986 WWF ® WWF registered
trademark owner

British Library Cataloguing in Publication Data
  Parker, Edward
  Birds. – (Rainforests)
  Rainforest animals   2. Birds
  I. Title
  598.1'724

ISBN 0 7502 4030 X

Printed in China by WKT

Hodder Children's Books
A division of Hodder Headline Limited
338 Euston Road, London NW1 3BH

CONTENTS

1 WELCOME TO THE RAINFOREST

◄ This brightly coloured taveta golden weaver bird is typical of many small birds that live in rainforest along coastal areas of East Africa.

THE RAINFOREST HOME

Birds live in all regions of the Earth, from the coldest places at the North and South Poles to the heat of the tropics. The rainforests lie around the Equator between the Tropics of Cancer and Capricorn, where temperatures are high all year round and the annual rainfall is greater than 2,000 mm. Tropical rainforests are found in parts of South and Central America, Africa, South-east Asia and Australasia. They are home to some of the world's most beautiful birds.

In the rainforests, there are more species of birds than in any other habitat on Earth. In the Amazon rainforest of South America, toucans and macaws fly high in the canopy while tiny hummingbirds dart from flower to flower. In the African rainforests, the screams of huge hornbills can be heard as they glide over the tallest trees. In Australasia, giant flightless birds called cassowaries race headlong through the vegetation on the forest floor. In South-east Asia, brilliantly coloured birds of paradise put on remarkable displays to their mates to show off their plumage.

Fascinating Fact

When a hummingbird hovers in front of a flower, it beats its wings so fast that it makes a humming sound.

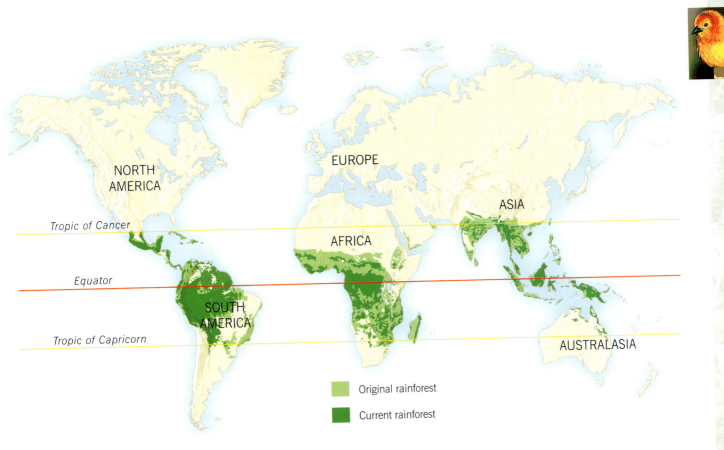

NORTH AMERICA

EUROPE

ASIA

AFRICA

Tropic of Cancer

Equator

SOUTH AMERICA

Tropic of Capricorn

AUSTRALASIA

Original rainforest

Current rainforest

▲ A map showing the extent of the world's tropical rainforests today, compared with their coverage 500 years ago, before large-scale deforestation began.

▼ Several species of macaws live in the Amazon rainforest. The scarlet macaw is one of the most brilliantly coloured birds of the Amazon.

THE VARIETY OF THE RAINFOREST

Rainforest birds share their rainforest home with many species of mammals, insects, spiders, reptiles and amphibians. They thrive on the plentiful plants and insects of the tropical rainforests. Of all the rainforest animals, birds are the most easily observed as they fly between the rainforest trees. This book will focus mainly on the variety of birds in the Amazon rainforest.

◀ *The lowland forest of the Amazon is home to a wide variety of birds, from eagles to parrots.*

TYPES OF RAINFOREST

Rainforests can be divided into two main types, according to their height above sea level. These are lowland forest and tropical montane forest. Lowland forests are the most widespread stretches of rainforest. They contain the majority of bird species, from parrots to giant monkey-eating eagles. Tropical montane forests occur on hills and mountains above 900 m, where conditions are generally cooler. The trees in these rainforests are typically shorter than in lowland forests and are often hidden in dense mists, giving rise to their alternative name, 'cloud forests'. The dense tangled vegetation of tropical montane forests is home to many unique species of birds such as pygmy owls and trogons. In South America, it is mainly in the tropical montane forests that the unique hummingbird is found.

▼ *Tropical montane forest is cooler than lowland forest and has different vegetation. Tropical montane forest is home to some unique species of birds.*

THE IMPORTANCE OF BIRDS

Birds are a vital part of the rainforest ecology and an important part of the food web. Predators such as eagles feed on small mammals, while flycatchers, which are perching birds, feed on insects.

RAINFOREST SECRETS

BIRDS OF PARADISE

There are 42 species of birds that are known as birds of paradise, and they are some of the most colourful birds in the rainforest.

Birds of paradise are found mainly in lowland forest in Papua New Guinea in South-east Asia. The group includes many birds with decorative feathers. The males show their colourful plumes when they dance to attract the females.

The male king bird of paradise lives in the tropical montane forest of Papua New Guinea in south-east Asia is typical of the species. The male bird is brightly coloured and has two wire-like tail feathers with a swirl of green barbs (decorative tufts) that are used in his courtship display as he swings upside down, calling to the females. The females choose their mates after watching the displays of the males.

Fascinating Fact

Parrots can easily grip fruits and nuts because their feet have opposing claws – two of their toes face forwards and two face backwards.

Birds also provide food for other rainforest animals. Many mammals, such as jaguars and monkeys, are predators and feed on birds and their eggs. Even some of the larger insects and spiders occasionally include small birds as part of their diet.

Many birds have lifestyles that are important for the survival of species of plants. Some birds, such as parrots and hummingbirds, help to pollinate rainforest flowers. Fruit-eating birds are also important in dispersing seeds. Toucans, parrots and quetzals eat fruit and carry the seeds, which they cannot digest, in their stomachs for many kilometres before expelling them.

② THE DIVERSITY OF BIRDS

◄ Some types of birds, such as gulls, are common throughout the world and different species can be found both in temperate and tropical climates.

THE RANGE OF BIRDS

There are many types of birds such as herons, gulls and vultures that are able to live in a wide variety of habitats around the world, including rainforests. However, many species of rainforest birds have evolved such specialized lifestyles that they can be found only in very small areas of particular rainforests. Hummingbirds, for example, have bills that are adapted to gaining nectar only from particular species of flowering rainforest plants.

Because of their ability to fly, birds have frequently colonized isolated rainforest islands. Over thousands of years, new species have evolved as birds adapted to their new surroundings. Where there were no predators, many island species evolved into flightless birds, such as the dodo and the cassowary bird, for example.

THE VARIETY OF BIRDS

The world's rainforests contain many of the estimated 8,600 species of birds that live on the Earth today. The colour of rainforest birds ranges from the dull browns of the nightjar to the brilliant

▼ The Papuan lorikeet is a colourful bird that lives on the island of Papua New Guinea.

RAINFOREST SECRETS

THE CASSOWARY BIRD

The cassowary (see right) is a very large flightless bird that lives in the rainforests of Australia, Papua New Guinea and Indonesia. It feeds mainly on fruits, berries and seeds from the forest floor.

Over millions of years, cassowaries have evolved to become flightless birds. Unlike almost all other birds, their wings are quite small and their bones are heavy. Cassowaries are well adapted to life on the ground. They have huge, muscular legs for fast running and sharp-toed feet for defence. A cassowary has a bald but brightly coloured head with a large horny ridge, which it holds forward to break the foliage ahead of it as it runs.

reds, greens and blues of hummingbirds and parrots. The wide variety of species and huge range of colours mask the fact that birds are the least varied of all groups of animals.

To enable them to fly, birds have remained fairly small and light compared with other animals. They have kept a similar basic shape, and their body structure is less varied than that of other groups, such as mammals.

◀ *Like the hummingbird, the bill of the pygmy honeyeater from Papua New Guinea is specially adapted for feeding on nectar.*

3 FEATURES OF A BIRD

A BIRD'S BODY

In many ways birds are similar to mammals. Like mammals, birds are descended from reptiles, and they are also warm-blooded. Birds also have four limbs like mammals, but these are made up of two legs and two wings. Sight and hearing are a bird's two main senses, and, like humans, a bird has a poor sense of smell. The main difference between mammals and birds is the way that birds have evolved for flight. Birds have developed huge flight muscles and a unique system of respiration. While mammals have lungs for breathing, birds use air sacs, as well as lungs. This greatly improves the flow of oxygen to their heart and wing muscles.

THE SKELETON

Over millions of years birds have gradually developed lightweight bones to help reduce their weight. Many of a bird's major bones such as its leg bones are hollow. Others have been greatly reduced in size to save weight.

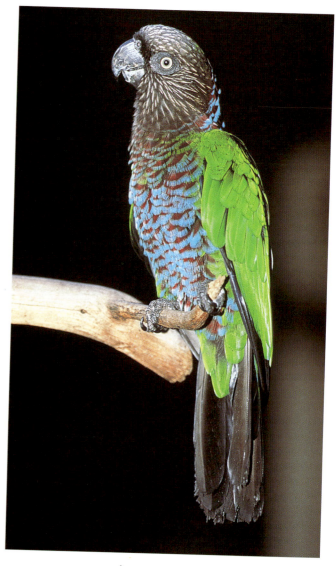

▲ An anaco parrot showing its features – feathers, wings, claws and a lightweight bill.

◄ The masked flower-piercer from the tropical montane forest of Ecuador. This bird has a bill designed to puncture the base of flowers. This enables it to feed on the nectar.

REPTILIAN BIRDS

The earliest fossil ever found of a bird-like creature is called the archaeopteryx. 'Archaeo' refers to ancient rocks and '–pteryx' means 'wing'. The 'fossil bird' was found in rocks in a quarry in Germany. The rocks date from the Jurassic period, around 160 million years ago.

This replica of the original fossil (see right) shows an animal that was halfway between a reptile and a bird. The head, jaw and tail were like those of a reptile, but it also had wings and feathers and could possibly fly. Because it had claws on its wings, many scientists believe that it probably clambered around in the trees and glided between them using its feather-covered wings and tail. It is believed that the bird's feathers developed from special reptile scales and evolved to help the bird keep warm.

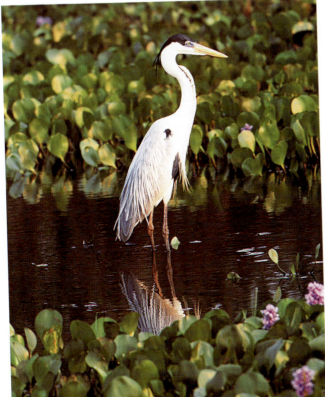

◀ *The hollow leg bones of large birds like herons help to reduce their weight, so making flying easier.*

Evolution has reduced the skull in size and weight to produce a lightweight head. Lightweight bills have replaced the heavy jawbones and teeth found in other animals. A bird's forelimbs, which are like the bones in the arms and fingers of humans, have been transformed into wings. Birds have evolved a very specialized breastbone, which is not only light but has a large surface area for the attachment of the bird's powerful wing muscles.

LUNGS AND HEART

The process of taking off, especially for large birds like herons and flamingoes, requires huge amounts of energy. The respiratory system of a bird allows it to breathe very efficiently. The bird's air sacs help to speed up the rate at which air enters the lungs. This system enables the bird to provide the necessary oxygen required by the heart and wing muscles during the stress of taking off. To assist, the heart is also capable of beating much faster than a mammal's heart and helps the blood to pump quickly around the body. The hearts of small tropical finches can reach rates of over 500 beats per minute, while the hearts of hummingbirds, can beat at over 1,250 beats per minute.

▼ *Flamingoes in Mexico's mangrove forest. These large birds require a huge amount of energy and plenty of oxygen to help them take off from the ground or from the water.*

RAINFOREST SECRETS

THE FEATHERS OF THE ARGUS PHEASANT

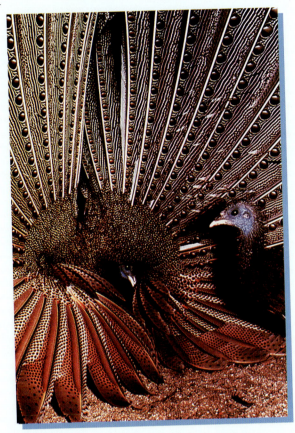

Argus pheasants live in the rainforests of Malaysia and have the largest feathers of any bird. Like the peacock, the argus pheasant has a magnificent tail display. The male attracts a female to a rainforest 'dancefloor' on a hill to show off its feathers. Towards the climax of the male's courtship dance, the argus pheasant reveals his plumage in all its glory. He throws up his wing feathers, revealing the previously hidden 'eyes' on his broad secondary feathers. The result is an almost three-dimensional impression of hundreds of 'eyes' looking at the chosen female.

WINGS AND FEATHERS

Feathers are one of the main features of birds, and they are strong and light. Each feather is made of a hollow central shaft, with lots of slender branches called barbs. The feathers on the back edge of the wing and the tail are the bird's longest feathers.

▲ *The secondary feathers on the head of this hummingbird are a beautiful shade of metallic green.*

They are called the primary feathers and they enable it to fly. The wings of small birds such as finches and thrushes are ideal for short flights between trees. Long wings, such as those of the frigate bird are designed for long-distance flights. Secondary feathers cover the whole body and provide a smooth surface, which helps reduce wind resistance. Air is also trapped beneath a bird's feathers forming a layer of insulation. Feathers of soft down grow under the secondary layer and help to keep the bird warm.

BILLS

Birds of different species have evolved a wide range of bills. Each bill is specially designed for a particular method of feeding. Each species of hummingbird, for example, has a bill that is specially designed to fit the shape of particular flowers it feeds on. Parrots have hugely powerful bills, which they use to crack nuts and tear unripe fruit. Some birds such as water hawks have strong, hooked bills that they use for tearing meat.

▶ *These brown pelicans use their huge bills to catch fish when they dive into the water.*

RAINFOREST SECRETS

TOUCAN BILLS

Toucans, that live in Central and South America, can have bills that grow longer than the rest of their bodies. Their bills are hard and sharp, but they are also thin and light.

For toucans, the colour of the bill is more important than the colour of the plumage because their bill helps to frighten away possible predators.

In the Amazon rainforest there are two species of toucan that like to eat food from the same trees. The stronger species defends the best fruit trees against competition from other birds. The weaker species, however, imitates the colouring of the bill and plumage of the larger one. Although it is a smaller bird, this makes it possible for it to feed in the trees of the stronger species. The weaker bird has to remain quiet so as not to give itself away with its different call.

Herons have long bills for catching fish in shallow water. The flamingo has a strange bill designed to sift small shellfish out of the mud at the bottom of lagoons. Some species of pelicans have huge bills, over 500 mm in length, which they use like a net to catch fish.

DIGESTION

The way birds eat and digest food, without the need for heavy jaws or teeth, has evolved to keep their bodies light for flying. Birds have a chamber in their throat, which is rather like a pouch. This is called a crop, or the first stomach. Food can be stored in the crop and also crushed down into smaller pieces. After being in the crop the food is passed to the gizzard, which is the second stomach. Once the food is inside the gizzard the muscles grind it up with the help of grit swallowed by the bird.

▼ *When eating, a parrot uses its feet to hold the fruit and its strong beak to tear the flesh away from the inner kernel.*

④ HOME AND HABITAT

◀ This black-fronted nunbird from South America lives deep in the rainforest. It finds a perch among the lower branches of the trees and watches for insects, which it catches in mid-air.

TYPES OF LOWLAND FOREST

Rainforests that are found in different parts of the world often look similar, but have unique conditions and species of birds that are not found anywhere else. The most widespread type of rainforest is lowland forest, such as exists in the Amazon basin. Here, the main division is between *terra firme* (dry ground) forest and *várzea* (flooded forest). The main feature of flooded forests is that they remain underwater for several months of each year. Another important type of lowland forest is mangrove forest, which is a specialized type of rainforest that lines about a quarter of all tropical coastlines.

▼ This smooth-billed ani from the lowland forest of the Amazon is not a strong flyer, and so feeds mainly on insects and fallen fruit on the forest floor.

RAINFOREST SECRETS

GUANS

Guans, such as the crested guan (see below), live in the drier parts of the lowland forest, from Mexico down to Brazil. Guans are mainly tree-dwelling birds. They can be seen moving in small groups across the treetops, although they will come to the ground to gorge on fallen fruit and to drink water. Guans can be easily heard because they have a loud, booming call that carries a long distance through the rainforest.

Male and female guans are very similar in appearance. During the mating season, the males perform a wing-drumming display, making a whirring sound to attract a mate. Once they are paired as breeding partners, guans usually make a bulky nest in the tallest tree they can find, to rear their young.

▲ Many species of parrots live in the terra firme forest of the Amazon, feeding on fruits and nuts.

DRY GROUND FOREST

In the Amazon rainforest, around four-fifths of the total area is *terra firme* forest. Crested guans, many types of parrots and toucans are just a few of the species living in *terra firme* forest. *Terra firme* forest also has species of trees and other plants that are not found in other types of rainforest. Some species of birds, such as the tyrian metaltail hummingbird and the hyacinth macaw, are specially adapted to feed on these trees and plants. Other bird species, such as the crested guan or the currasow, survive on very specific types of fruits, seeds and leaves found only in the *terra firme* forest.

17

▲ The changing water level of the flooded forest provides ideal conditions for birds that feed on fish, such as herons and egrets.

FLOODED FOREST

Flooded forests occur in rainforests all around the world, but the largest and most famous example is the flooded forest in the upper Amazon, near the city of Manaus, in Brazil. Here the water levels fall and rise between the dry and wet seasons, so the area is completely flooded in the wet season. The types of trees that can survive this flooding are very different from those that are found in the *terra firme* forests. The flooded forest provides a wide range of habitats from large trees where birds such as hoatzins feed, to

RAINFOREST SECRETS

THE HOATZIN

Hoatzins (see below right) are unusual birds that have evolved uniquely in the flooded forest of the Amazon river basin. Because there is little dry land, the young hoatzins have three hooks where their wings bend to help them remain in the trees. These hooks act like claws when they are moving through the rainforest branches. Young hoatzins also have claws on their first and second toes, which they use to grasp the trees. This helps them to move like tree-living lizards through the flooded forest.

Hoatzins feed on waterside vegetation. They eat the new leaves, flowers and fruits of trees such as cecropia and black mangrove. Their digestive system is specially

adapted to process leaves that other animals cannot digest. A hoatzin's crop is fifty times larger than its second stomach, where its diet of tough leaves is further digested.

shallow wetlands where a variety of herons and ibises catch food. The larger waterways are ideal for anhingas (snakebirds) and kingfishers.

MANGROVE FOREST

Mangrove forest grows in mud at the edges of seas and rivers. Mangrove forest is made up of trees with 'breathing' roots to overcome the wet, salty conditions. These roots stick out above the water line and allow the trees to take in oxygen from the air. Mangrove forests are home to many species of birds and are particularly important for nesting seabirds and migrating flocks. Plenty of fish lay their eggs here, so many fish-eating birds live in the mangrove forests. Birds such as the mangrove hummingbird, the frigate bird and many species of wading birds live in this type of habitat.

▲ The anu from Brazil spends much of its time close to the edge of rivers and among mangrove roots.

TROPICAL MONTANE FOREST

There are many species of birds that live in tropical montane forest. It is home to various species of trogons, owls, vultures, hummingbirds and ant pitas. The trees are covered in many types of plants called epiphytes, including orchids and bromeliads. Birds such as hummingbirds feed on the nectar of these rainforest flowers. Many of the species of hummingbirds that live in these habitats are very rare because so little untouched tropical montane forest remains.

◄ The rufus-naped brush finch is found only in the tropical montane forests of Ecuador and Colombia.

5 LIFESTYLES

DIVISIONS BY LIFESTYLE

Birds are often divided into groups that have similar lifestyles or distinctive features. Birds of prey, parrots, gamebirds, pigeons and hummingbirds are just a few examples of the major groups of birds that live in the rainforests. Species of many of these groups are also found in other parts of the world. For example, it is possible to see different species of gulls in the Amazon rainforest, northern Europe and North America. Herons, storks and kingfishers are other types of birds where different species can be found both in the tropical rainforest and in temperate parts of the world. The lifestyles of the main groups of rainforest birds are explained in this chapter.

▼ Vultures are commonly seen within the rainforests, but are also found scavenging in towns and villages.

BIRDS OF PREY

Birds of prey include vultures, eagles, kites, buzzards, falcons and fish eagles, such as the endangered African fish eagle from West Africa. Some of the world's largest species of birds, such as the king vulture, are birds of prey.

THE HARPY EAGLE

The harpy eagle is the world's largest eagle and is found in areas of untouched rainforest throughout Central and South America. This harpy eagle chick (see right) is from the Amazon rainforest in Peru. Each of its feet will grow to the size of a man's hand, and its lethally sharp talons will be used to grab its prey. The fully grown harpy eagle usually hits its prey at high speed, often killing it outright with the impact.

The harpy eagle mainly feeds on monkeys, sloths, coatimundis, opossums and tree porcupines. It has unusually short wings for a bird of its size, allowing it to fly more easily between the dense rainforest trees.

▼ Despite their small size, scops owls are excellent hunters, preying on nocturnal mammals in the rainforests of Madagascar.

All birds, from giant vultures to the tiny pygmy African falcons, share a number of specialized features. These include powerful legs, feet with sharp claws, superb eyesight and a hooked bill. Many rainforest eagles, hawks and owls are formidable hunters, while vultures are expert in scavenging the prey of other animals. Most birds of prey, such as the monkey-eating eagle, kill their victim with their claws. They can strike a sloth or monkey at great speed, often killing it immediately. A few species of eagles, however, kill their prey outright by a blow directly from their sharp, hooked bill.

Fascinating Fact

The crowned eagle can snatch monkeys from trees and small antelopes from the forest floor.

THE PARROT FAMILY

There are 330 species of parrot worldwide. They can be divided into three families – parrots, lorikeets (lories) and cockatoos, although cockatoos are not usually found in the rainforest.

PARROTS

This family of parrots includes macaws, parrots and parakeets (small parrots). The parrot family is found mainly in the rainforests of Australia, South America and South-east Asia. It includes many brilliantly coloured birds that squawk and chatter loudly as they fly above the rainforest. They nest in tree hollows and feed largely on fruit, seeds, nectar and fungi. They have highly specialized bills that they use for cracking nuts and tearing open fruit. Their bill can also be used as a 'third foot', for holding on when climbing among a tree's branches.

◀ *The chestnut-fronted, parrot, sometimes called the severe parrot, is found throughout the rainforests of the Americas, from Panama to Bolivia.*

MACAWS

The macaw is a brightly coloured bird, found only in South America. It is the largest type of parrot and can measure almost a metre from its head to the tip of its tail. In the wild, macaws are among the noisiest of all birds with their constant chatter of loud and tuneless squawks, shrieks and clicks. Macaws are intelligent and playful and can be taught to mimic.

The scarlet macaw (see above) is one of the largest and most striking types of macaw. The scarlet macaws form breeding pairs for life, which can be longer than thirty years. Like most parrots they feed on fruits, nuts and berries and nest in the hollows of trees.

► *All types of parrots, such as these hyacinth macaws, tend to group together and nest in the hollows of large trees.*

Fascinating Fact

The top and bottom of a macaw's beak rub together to keep the edges sharp.

▼ *The black-capped lorikeet lives on the island of Papua New Guinea.*

Many parakeets are fast fliers and South American macaws are excellent fliers even though they are larger than parakeets. While the macaws are usually multi-coloured, most parrots tend to be mainly green.

LORIKEETS

The lorikeets form a distinct sub-group within the parrot family. There are over 50 species of lorikeets, most of which occur throughout the rainforests of Indonesia, Papua New Guinea, Australia and the islands of the Pacific. Lorikeets are treetop birds and tend to fly in large, noisy groups between flowering trees. Like macaws, they are brightly coloured and they are generally smaller than most parrots. However, the feature that sets them apart from the other types of parrot is their brush-like tongue, which they use to extract nectar and pollen from rainforest flowers.

Lorikeets are well known for their theatrical displays as well as for their stunning plumage. The rainbow lorikeet, for example, has up to thirty special gestures such as hopping, walking and preening, which it uses in its dances. These displays are used to frighten off other males and attract females to mate.

GAMEBIRDS

There are 263 species of gamebirds worldwide. This group includes pheasants and currasows. In the rainforests of Africa and South-east Asia these birds live mainly on the ground, where they can find plenty of food. In South and Central America, they prefer to live in the trees because there is more food in the trees than on the forest floor. Gamebirds, with their rounded bodies, are hunted for food by rainforest people. In other parts of the world gamebirds are domesticated. These species of birds are closely related to the rainforest varieties.

PHEASANTS

There are over 150 species of pheasants worldwide. Pheasants can be divided into three main groups: partridges, quails and true pheasants. Pheasants usually have plump, rounded bodies, powerful wings and long, unfeathered legs. Most pheasants can only fly short distances and live on the ground, scratching about for seeds to eat. Most species are

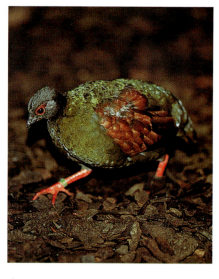

▲ Gamebirds have a similar basic shape, with a rounded body, strong wings and long legs. This is the female roulroul partridge from South-east Asia.

◄ It is fairly common among species of pheasants for the male to be quite different in colour from the female. This male roulroul is also clearly identified by his red, brush-like crest.

RAINFOREST SECRETS

RED JUNGLE FOWL

One rainforest bird that is familiar to millions of people who do not live near the rainforest is the red jungle fowl. This is the ancestor of the domestic chicken and originally inhabited many parts of South-east Asia. Like many other types of pheasants, the male red jungle fowl has striking plumage. It displays feathers in a wide range of colours such as iridescent green, gold and chestnut and has a brilliant red, fleshy comb on its head. The less colourful females are varying shades of brown and chestnut.

Like other pheasants from Africa and South-east Asia, the red jungle fowl is a ground-living bird, usually seen in large groups. Flocks of jungle fowl spend much of their time scratching around on the forest floor looking for insects, seeds, fallen fruit and young shoots.

found in South-east Asia but a few species are found in Africa. The types of pheasants that are found in these different parts of the world include the Congo peacock, the red jungle fowl of Sumatra and Java, the argus pheasant of Malaysia and the roulroul partridge of Sumatra and Borneo.

CURRASOWS

Currasows are a group of 44 species of gamebirds (including guans) that live in the rainforests of South and Central America.

Although they live mainly in the trees, and will only occasionally visit the forest floor to collect fallen fruit, currasows are large birds that appear clumsy when moving about in the high branches. The great currasow is typical of this group of birds. Like guans, currasows are well known for their booming calls. The calls of the nocturnal currasow can be heard echoing through the rainforest at night. There is one currasow known as a chacalaca because of its unusual three-syllable call.

PIGEONS

There are over 300 species of pigeons (including doves) in this family, many of which are rainforest species. One of the most famous species of pigeon was the dodo, a giant flightless bird that lived on the island of Mauritius, over 300 years ago. Dodos died out when they became a target for the visiting Dutch sailors looking for an easy meal. Also, rats and dogs from the sailors' ships ate the dodo's eggs or killed their chicks. Because of this, dodos eventually became extinct by 1681.

Today, most types of rainforest pigeons are found in Australia and South-east Asia and can vary greatly in size. Species include the bleeding heart dove and the Victoria crested pigeon. Both male and female pigeons are unique because they secrete a milky substance from the lining of their crop to feed their young for the first few days.

▼ *A dove finds food, such as seeds and fruit, on the forest floor.*

THE BLUE CROWNED PIGEON

The blue crowned pigeon is native to the rainforests of north-west Papua New Guinea, where it lives in muddy lowland forest. The blue crowned pigeon is among the largest of the pigeon groups. On its head it has a beautiful, distinctive crest of fan-shaped, lacy feathers.

Like all members of the pigeon family, the males and females are very similar in appearance, but display very different courtship behaviour. Pigeons live together in small groups and form mating pairs for life, which is unusual for ground-living birds. Both parents take their turn in sitting on the two eggs that are laid, until they hatch 28 days later.

▲ A hummingbird, hovering at nectar-producing flowers to feed. Hummingbirds also catch mosquitoes and other small insects as part of their diet.

Fascinating Fact

Hummingbirds have special wing muscles that allow them to beat their wings at up to 80 beats per second.

HUMMINGBIRDS

There are 320 species of hummingbirds in South America. Because of their size and body structure, they form a unique group. Most species are very small; the frilled coquette from Brazil, for example, weighs less than 3g. Many species of hummingbirds are well adapted to living in the rainforest. At 120 mm in length, the sword-billed hummingbird has the longest bill of any bird, in relation to its body. This allows it to probe the nectar deep in the trumpet-shaped flowers it feeds on in the tropical montane forest of Venezuela. Hummingbirds are exceptional fliers. They are able to fly forwards, sideways and backwards, hover and even fly upside down.

WATER AND WADING RAINFOREST BIRDS

Many rainforest bird species are adapted to living beside waterways and lakes. These groups of birds include herons, ducks, kingfishers, darters, cormorants, storks and many other types of waders and gulls. In the Amazon rainforest, water and wading birds take advantage of the great changes in the level of the water between the seasons. Large flocks of birds can be seen around small lakes, where fish become trapped in the dry season.

HERONS

There are over 60 species of herons worldwide. Rainforest herons are medium-to-large sized birds. They have long necks and legs, slim bodies and broad wings. Herons hunt in water of varying depth. They can wade or remain motionless, catching fish and other creatures in their dagger-shaped bills. Herons have special down feathers on their chests, which produce a powder. After feeding, this powder is used to clean the greasy marks left on their chests from catching and eating fish.

◀ *(Above left) An Amazonian moorhen is a waterbird that is common along the waterways of the Amazon rainforest.*

▲ *(Above right) Herons are wading birds that move slowly through the shallows, waiting to snatch small fish with their long bills.*

RAINFOREST SECRETS

THE JACANA WATERBIRDS

This family of waterbirds is easy to identify because all the birds have very large feet in relation to their bodies. Jacanas have evolved very long toes and claws, which help them distribute their weight over wide areas. This helps jacanas to move over floating plants such as lilies, and has given rise to their alternative name, 'lily-trotters'.

In the Amazon rainforest, jacanas usually feed on small fish, insects and seeds of aquatic plants. Although they are poor fliers they are excellent at swimming and diving.

The jacanas are well camouflaged by their colour as they move among the floating vegetation.

 These Amazonian pato da cristas are found in large flocks on lakes and slow-moving rivers throughout the Amazon rainforest.

DUCKS

There are more than 140 species of ducks worldwide, many of which live in the rainforests. The wet conditions are ideal for many species of ducks that obtain plant and animal food either from the surface of the water or from the bottom of a lake or river. Rainforest species include the large muscovy duck and the pato da crista, which can often be seen in large flocks in the Amazon.

CORMORANTS

There are around 30 species of cormorants worldwide and they are found in many different habitats, including the rainforests. The reed cormorant, for example, lives in West Africa and Madagascar. Like other cormorants it is a fairly large, web-footed bird with a strongly hooked bill. A shag is another name for a cormorant.

DARTERS

There are four species of darters, all of which are tropical varieties, found in South and Central America. Both cormorants and darters specialize in catching fish. Both dive into the water with their wings held to their sides in order to catch their prey. From the surface they sometimes dive deep underwater, paddling downwards using their webbed feet. Cormorants and darters are commonly seen drying off on perches at the edge of rivers and lakes.

▲ *The long-tailed shag is a member of the cormorant family and lives along the rainforest rivers of Cameroon and Nigeria in Africa.*

RAINFOREST SECRETS

THE AMAZONIAN SNAKEBIRD

The anhinga is a type of darter that lives along the edges of rivers throughout the Amazon rainforest. Locally, it is called a snakebird because when it is swimming only its head and long neck can be seen above the water. From its swimming position, it usually dives to over 5 m underwater. Darters have evolved a body that is not designed to float well, so it can dive more effectively.

When the snakebird has finished diving for food, it comes to the surface to dry off. Like other types of cormorants or darters, snakebirds are a common sight on perches at the edge of rivers and lakes, sitting with their wings spread out, drying in the sun.

▼ *Kingfishers like to find a perch above a river, from where they dive to catch small fish and insects.*

KINGFISHERS

There are 86 species of kingfishers worldwide. Most of these are tropical varieties and are brightly coloured. Kingfishers have a distinctive bill that is always straight, with a pointed tip. Many kingfishers catch fish and insects by diving from a perch above the water. However, most species of kingfishers feed on dry land catching snakes, insects and lizards. They usually nest in burrows along the banks of rivers.

Like this bird, many species of birds of paradise are in danger of becoming extinct in the wild because of the effects of deforestation.

Fascinating Fact

In 2001, Friends of the Earth estimated that 60 per cent of all rainforest timber entering the UK came from illegal sources.

Many species of rainforest birds have been pushed to the brink of extinction over the last hundred years. It is likely that many of the rarest birds will no longer exist in the wild before the end of the twenty-first century. The glaucous macaw from South America has already become extinct. There are many reasons for the decline in rainforest species, but they are mainly caused by the activities of humans. These include habitat destruction, introducing new forms of agriculture, pollution, hunting birds for food, collecting birds for the pet trade and indirectly killing birds by introducing predators.

An area of tropical montane forest that has been cut down and is beginning to regenerate. The renewed rainforest will not support the same variety of bird species as the original rainforest.

HABITAT DESTRUCTION

It is estimated that 400,000 hectares of rainforest in the Amazon are being cut down each year (source: UNEP/WCMC) to produce timber, firewood, charcoal and wood pulp for paper. Vast areas are also being converted into agricultural land. Soya bean production in the Amazon

Hornbills

There are many different species of hornbill in the rainforests of Africa and South-east Asia. They include the helmeted hornbill and wreathed hornbill (see right) of South-east Asia and the pied hornbill of West Africa. Many species of hornbill have a distinctive long bill with an extension that resembles a horn.

Several species of hornbill are severely affected by logging. Hornbills make their nests in mature trees, but these trees may be burned when the best timber from the rainforest is removed.

Research in West Africa has shown that as soon as a new logging road is cut through an area of primary rainforest in countries like Sierra Leone, species such as the pied hornbill retreat into another patch of untouched forest. This means that large parts of the African rainforest no longer contain hornbills.

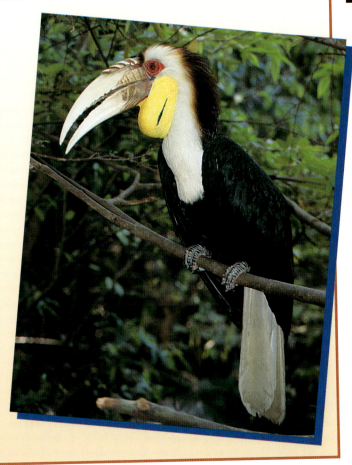

rainforest, African oil palm plantations in West Africa and rice cultivation in South-east Asia have caused the loss of millions of hectares of rainforest. Building dams,

▼ Making way for cattle ranches has had a severe affect on birds in South and Central America.

digging mines and the expansion of towns and cities have also led to rainforest loss. As rainforests are reduced to smaller and smaller fragments bird species not only disappear, but the migration routes of many birds also become disrupted.

Rainforest birds are harmed by changes to their habitat. The draining of wetlands to create new farmland means that waterfowl and wading birds no longer have homes. Logging removes many of the large trees where parrots and birds of prey breed. The burning of the fallen timber affects those species that feed on the insects and fungi that live in decaying logs.

EGGS, FEATHERS AND SKINS

Many rainforest bird species are highly prized for their eggs, feathers and even their skins. In the eighteenth and nineteenth centuries, for example, it was fashionable to wear shawls made of hummingbird skins. Egg collectors have also drastically reduced the wild populations of birds such as eagles and parrots. It takes a long time for these birds to become old enough to lay eggs and when they are of breeding age they lay only a few eggs each year. Feathers have also been fashionable during recent years, and many species including the birds of paradise are still trapped for their valuable plumage and smuggled in huge numbers to the USA and Europe.

THE PET TRADE

The capture of rainforest birds for the pet trade has had a serious effect on the numbers of certain species. Parrots are just one example of birds that have been caught in their thousands to provide pets for people. Now there are fewer than 500 parrots of the St Lucia species in the Caribbean left, because they have been captured for the pet trade. The African Grey parrot is also threatened. It is one of the most popular and talkative of parrots. It lives in large groups in the rainforests of West, Central and East Africa. The birds roost together on tall trees along the edges of lakes and follow regular routes to and from their roosts each day. Their habits in the wild make the African Greys easy to catch.

▲ *Colourful feathers are collected from trapped birds as fashionable items.*

▶ *Parrots are popular pets throughout the world. This woman from Ecuador shows how tame her pet is.*

RAINFOREST SECRETS

CAGED BIRDS

The first record of a caged parrot occurred in Greece around 400 BC. Ever since then parrots have been popular as pets, especially as they are able to mimic speech in various languages. Soon after the Americans discovered tropical parrots living in South and Central America, they were exported to collectors in Europe.

This fascination for caged parrots has continued up until the present day. It has led to a huge reduction in the number of birds in the rainforests. The international trade in birds has lessened in the last twenty years, but in many developing countries it is part of the local culture to have a caged bird in the home.

In Brazil, Costa Rica, Thailand, Liberia and in many other countries, rainforest birds are still being caught and sold in large numbers.

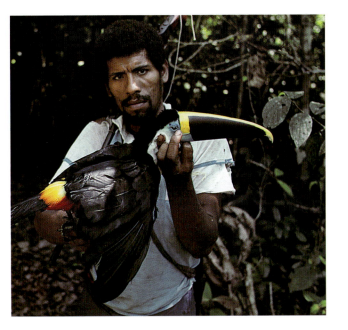

HUNTING

Rainforest birds are hunted for a living and for sport. In many poor countries, bird meat provides protein for rural families. In Brazil, both toucans and ducks are hunted for food. In many cultures shooting a bird of prey is a ritual part of growing up. Tourists also kill some birds for sport, while birds of prey are shot on sight by farmers who mistakenly think that all birds will attack their animals.

◀ *In remote areas, rainforest people hunt birds like this toucan to supplement their meagre diets.*

◀ Pollution and the production of vast quantities of rubbish from rainforest cities is affecting local bird populations. Some birds disappear, while scavengers like vultures often increase in number.

POLLUTION

Many birds are at the top of the food chain and feed on other creatures, such as insects. Because they are controlled by pesticides such as DDT, insects often have poisonous chemicals inside their bodies, which are then eaten by predatory birds. Such chemicals are known to affect the breeding of hawks and falcons, causing their eggshells to be thinner. They can also affect rainforest birds by killing insects, which are their main food. Pollution in the air, especially poisonous metals such as lead and cadmium from cars and pollution from industry, is also known to build up on the wing feathers of birds. This is taken into the body when a bird preens itself.

▼ Millions of square kilometres of rainforest have been destroyed by fire as people convert the rainforest into agricultural land. This kills off insects that are an important food for birds.

AGRICULTURE

Converting areas of rainforest to plantations for agriculture can have serious effects on local bird populations. The setting up of large oil palm plantations in Cameroon, for example, has created 'avian deserts', where only a few rainforest birds can continue to survive. Chemicals are often used to poison birds that try and feed on the crops. Burning the forest floor to prepare land for agriculture can kill off insects such as army ants, but these are vital foods to ant birds and other species of rainforest birds.

Agricultural Projects

Developing large-scale agricultural projects in rainforest areas has led to the numbers of birds declining rapidly. These create areas of 'avian desert'.

African oil palm plantations usually occupy land that was once teeming with a huge variety of bird species. Few birds feed on oil palm, and those that do are trapped or shot to ensure the best harvest for the farmers. In this way many species of rainforest bird lose both their source of food and their home. Every few years, plantations are cleared of oil palms and they become deserted areas (see right) while the ground recovers.

Many birds that live deep inside the rainforest are affected by the service roads and other open spaces caused by the creation of plantations.

This is because birds do not like to fly across open spaces between areas of forest. Eventually, groups of birds become isolated from others in small pockets of rainforest.

INTRODUCTION OF ALIEN SPECIES

Many species of rainforest bird are affected by the introduction of new predators. This has been particularly serious on rainforest islands where the introduction of domestic animals has led to the extinction of local birds. They are easily wiped out by the introduction of rats, pigs and cats who prey on the birds, their young or their eggs. Introducing other bird species may also be devastating for local birds. The parasitic shiny cowbird, for example, was introduced in the West Indies. This is a bird that pushes eggs out of other birds' nests, which has caused a serious decline in the local population of other birds.

By observing birds in the rainforests, scientists are trying to learn more about their behaviour and habitat in order to help protect them.

SAVING BIRDS

The wild populations of many rainforest birds such as the St Lucia parrot and African fish eagle are critically low. Without help, these rainforest birds could become extinct within the next 30 years. Fortunately, there are many individuals and organizations that are working hard to help conserve the rainforests and the rare bird species that live in them. WWF, Birdlife International and the International Union of Bird Preservation (IUBP), and other organizations are all campaigning hard for the protection of rainforest habitats and endangered bird species.

Fascinating Fact

There are 47 threatened parrot species in South America and the Caribbean, and three in Africa and Madagascar.

▼ A hummingbird is caught in a mist net. Researchers can weigh, measure and tag the bird as part of their research before releasing it.

RESEARCH

Research into bird numbers and the way birds live in the rainforest is a vital part of conservation. It is only by understanding the way that birds survive that proper conservation measures can be undertaken. Hummingbirds, for example, rely on only a few species of flowers for food.

▼ *Conservation organizations are campaigning against large-scale projects because they cause so much damage to the habitats of rainforest birds.*

Many species of parrots need a particular species of tree for their nesting sites. These trees must be allowed to mature enough to provide hollows to nest in. Many species of birds will not cross open areas such as created by oil pipelines and roads. They need stretches of rainforest, or rainforest corridors, to link fragments of rainforest to each other.

LINKS

The Rio Mazan Project

In 1986 a water company in Ecuador, which owned an area of tropical montane forest close to the city of Cuenca, allowed a team of scientists to carry out a bird survey in the rainforest to identify the bird species present.

Like these researchers inspecting a hummingbird (see right), they recorded information about the birds before releasing each one. In the course of their survey, they observed some very rare species of birds including Andean toucans, ant pitas, trogons and even Andean condors.

The results of the bird survey and the other research showed that although the area of rainforest was quite small, it had many species of birds that had disappeared from other parts of the Andes. When the surrounding habitat was destroyed, many birds had flown to this area of tropical montane forest, making it their home and so producing a wide range of species in a small area. The outcome was the protection of the area for birds.

This group of children from Colombia are trying to help local bird species. They are replanting trees and creating rainforest corridors, linking patches of isolated rainforest.

Fascinating Fact

The Brazilian government has pledged to triple the area of protected rainforest in the Amazon to 25 million hectares.

▼ Some local people, such as this craftsman from Brazil, make souvenirs that appeal to people interested in rainforest birds.

SHARING THE RAINFOREST

For many indigenous peoples, such as the Yanomami of Brazil or the Baka pygmies of Cameroon, sharing the rainforest with animals and birds is part of their culture and their religious beliefs. However, most of the world's economy is based on exploiting resources as quickly and as cheaply as possible with little thought for the future or the needs of the other living creatures that people share the world with.

Many conservation organizations, such as WWF, have been campaigning for governments, businesses and individuals to use rainforest resources carefully, so as not to cause damage to the environment. Many logging companies have changed their practices. They now often only harvest the most valuable trees in the rainforest. The rest of the rainforest, which used to be felled and burned, is left standing for the benefit of the local wildlife and people.

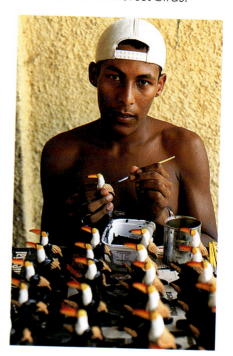

The Hyacinth Macaw

The hyacinth macaw is one of the rarest parrots in Brazil, with a population of about 3,000 birds. It is one of the world's largest and most colourful parrots. Around half of these macaws live in the Amazon rainforest. The hyacinth macaw is a brilliant blue colour and is easily seen as it flies between its favourite palm trees, searching for food. It is now so rare that tourists come from all over the world to see it in its natural habitat.

The hyacinth macaw is an ideal species to attract ecotourists to the Amazon rainforest.

Part of the money that comes from tourism can be used to help preserve the mature trees that the hyacinth macaw likes to nest in.

ECOTOURISM

Tourists will travel thousands of kilometres to see rare rainforest birds in their natural habitat. The industry that has developed, based around tourism, helps conservation in two ways. First, the governments of rainforest countries are reminded that their wildlife, including birds, attracts tourists and this has an economic value. Second, it shows that there are alternatives to damaging activities such as logging and cattle ranching. Ecotourism may encourage rainforest nations to slow down habitat destruction and help to protect the homes of rare bird species.

◀ *In some rainforest towns and cities, the value of the local wildlife is recognized and featured in unusual ways.*

PROTECTED AREAS

Some species of birds such as hornbills, harpy eagles and parrots need large areas of rainforest in order to lead natural lives. Many rainforest birds also need to stop off in rainforest areas and wetlands when migrating to their breeding grounds. Organizations such as WWF have successfully campaigned for protected areas of rainforest to be set up all over the world. These can take the form of national parks, nature reserves, community managed land, rainforest reserves and certified rainforest areas. WWF has been campaigning for more rainforest corridors to link these protected areas.

INTERNATIONAL LAW

Over the last few decades, many rare bird species have been given much more protection by introducing new international and national laws. In many countries, there are laws that aim to stop the hunting of rare birds for the pet trade and the collection of eggs.

▲ Birds that migrate long distances, such as pelicans, need areas of protected rainforest along the routes where they fly.

◄ The setting up of protected areas such as this area of rainforest in Australia will help to ensure the future for many types of rainforest birds.

Fascinating Fact

A new species of owl has recently been discovered in Ecuador in South America.

Lago Mamiraua

The ecological station called Lago Mamiraua in the Amazon rainforest is a vast area of flooded forest that is now protected and managed for the benefit of both the wildlife and the local population. It covers 1,124,000 hectares and is home to a variety of rare and endangered birds including the hoatzin, the very rare umbrella bird and the great currasow.

Initially funded by WWF, the project at the ecological station has been so successful at improving the quality of life for the small rainforest communities and conserving the endangered wildlife that it is now used as a model in other parts of the Amazon rainforest.

▼ *A weaver bird in the Korup National Rainforest park, a protected area in Cameroon in West Africa.*

There are also special international laws to prevent skins, feathers, bills and other bird products from rare birds being traded around the world. The setting up of RAMSAR world heritage sites for the protection of important wetlands has given a number of rare migratory and wading birds a chance of survival.

Most countries around the world have signed the United Nations' International Convention on Biological Diversity. This is an agreement to help protect rare species from becoming extinct.

8 THE FUTURE

AN UNCERTAIN FUTURE

The future of many rainforest birds is uncertain. Many species such as the Spix's macaw may be reduced to living in captivity in tiny numbers. It is likely that many rainforests will be destroyed in the next thirty years, and many species will no longer be able to survive in the wild.

Despite the efforts of environmental organizations and individuals the only chance of long-term survival for many rainforest species lies in a change in attitude towards the way rainforests are used. However, more demands are being made on rainforest resources as the world's population increases. Most rainforests occur in the world's poorest countries, which often have little option but to exploit their natural resources to earn the money needed for development and repaying debt.

ASSISTING BIRDS

There are a number of ways the future of rainforest birds can be helped and assisted. These include reducing the numbers of birds caught for the pet trade, buying timber

◄ *(Above left) This parrot species is being bred in captivity. Captive breeding helps to ensure that even if the species becomes extinct in the wild, a few birds will continue to exist.*

▲ *(Above right) Many species of macaws are now endangered. Action now could help protect the unique habitats in which they live and could prevent many other species from becoming extinct.*

Fascinating Fact

In 1990 only one Spix's macaw remained in the wild in Brazil.

QUETZAL – GOD OF THE AIR

The quetzal is one of the most striking birds of Central and South America. It has a glittering emerald-green tail and wing feathers and a crimson front on its lower body. Its magnificent tail has two curving plumes that can reach almost a metre in length.

For ancient tribes of Central America, such as the Aztecs, the quetzal was considered to be divine and it was worshipped as god of the air. Only the royal family was allowed to wear its tail feathers, which were removed from the live birds. Any common person who killed a quetzal was put to death.

The number of quetzals in the wild has dropped dramatically as the tropical montane forests have been cleared in its home range from southern Mexico to Panama, and because it has been hunted for souvenirs. The quetzal is the national bird of Mexico, and needs protection because of its rarity and its fascinating history.

from plantations rather than from rainforests and creating protected areas for rainforest birds to live in. The development of ecotourism, such as birding holidays, is another way of protecting the birds' rainforest habitat and it also provides local people with a means of earning money.

Many economic activities that take place in the rainforests could have far less impact on the environment and the species that live in them. There are many less destructive economic activities than the large-scale logging, ranching and agriculture practices that happen today. However, many of these activities are driven by the demands of the world's wealthiest countries. It is not only up to local people and governments but also up to people and companies in the richest countries to alter their activities so that rainforest bird species and other rainforest wildlife can be offered a better future.

► *Understanding more about rainforest birds helps us to find ways of protecting them.*

45

GLOSSARY

Jabiru stork.

air sacs Special thin-walled structures linked to the lungs that help improve respiration in birds.

alien An organism that is located in an area that is not its usual habitat.

bromeliads A group of plants that comes from the Americas and has a rosette of spiny leaves.

camouflage Colours, shapes and patterns that help any living thing blend in with its surroundings.

courtship display Special behaviour such as a dance or display of feathers used by some species of birds to attract a mate.

crop A chamber or pouch, used by birds to store food in order to carry it back to the nest.

ecological station Under Brazilian law this is an area where both the traditional activities of the local people and the wildlife are protected.

ecotourism Encouraging people to visit an area because of its beauty and natural wildlife.

epiphytes Plants that grow on other plants.

evolved When a species of any organism has changed by natural processes over many generations.

extinct Died out. When the species of any organism no longer exists.

fossils The remains of organisms from millions of years ago, preserved in solid rock.

fungi A group of non-flowering plants, such as mushrooms or moulds. They usually live on other plants.

habitat The natural home of living things.

insulation When an animal or bird has a layer of fur or feathers to prevent the loss of body heat.

migration When a living thing makes a seasonal journey to a new habitat.

nocturnal To be active mainly at night.

pesticides Substances that can be used to kill fungi, bacteria or insects.

plumage The pattern and colours created by the feathers on a bird.

pollinate When pollen is transferred from the male to the female parts of the flower.

predators Living things that regularly prey on others for food.

preening When a bird cleans or tidies its feathers with its bill, to keep them in good order.

RAMSAR An international agreement concerned with the protection of wetland areas.

respiration system The heart, lungs and blood vessels that work together to keep the blood oxygenated.

roost When birds perch to go to sleep.

species A group of organisms, such as insects, plants, animals or birds that closely resemble one another.

wetland An area of land that remains waterlogged for most of the year.

wind resistance The 'pull' that slows a bird down when it tries to move quickly through the air.

URTHER INFORMATION

BOOKS TO READ

A River Journey: The Amazon by Simon Scoones (Hodder Wayland, 2003)

Journey into the Rainforest by Tim Knight (Oxford University Press, 2001)

Rainforest Birds by Bobbie Kalman (Crabtree Publishing, 1998)

Secrets of the Rainforest by Michael Chinery (Cherrytree, 2001)

Survivor's Science in the Rainforest by Peter Riley (Hodder Wayland, 2003)

Up a Rainforest Tree by Rod Theodorou and Carole Telford (Heinnemann Library, 1998)

WEBSITES

BirdLife International
http://www.birdlife.org.uk/
A global alliance network with projects worldwide. Priorities including saving species, their habitats and working with communities towards sustainability.

Passport to the Rainforest
http://www.passporttoknowledge.com/rainforest/main.html
Includes maps, graphics, images and information about plants and animals.

Rainforest Action Network
http://www.ran.org/
Facts about rainforest people and animals presented in a question and answer format. Includes action that children can take to conserve the rainforests.

Conservation International
http://www.conservation.org/
Provides species data for plants and animals including news, projects and articles.

Forest Conservation
http://www.forests.org/
News, information, ecology and conservation. Includes a links page for children.

Species Survival Network CITES Conference
http://www.defenders.org/cites
Information on CITES conferences, which discuss the world's endangered species.

World Rainforest Movement
http://www.wrm.org.uy/
Includes information on rainforests by country and by subject.

WWF–UK
http://www.wwf.org.uk/
In addition to its main website in the UK, the environmental organization has a number of sites:
http://www.panda.org/
The international site for WWF.
http://www.panda.org/forests4life
The forests for life campaign.

The website addresses (URLs) included in this book were valid at the time of going to press. However, because of the nature of the Internet, it is possible that some addresses may have changed, or sites may have changed or closed down since publication. While the authors and Publishers regret any inconvenience this may cause the readers, no responsibility for any such changes can be accepted by either the author or the Publisher.

ADDRESSES OF ORGANIZATIONS

BirdLife International, Wellbrook Court, Girton Road, Cambridge CB3 ONA Tel: 01223 277318
http://www.birdlife.org.uk/
Chester Zoo, Chester GH2 1LH Tel: 01244 380280
http://www.chesterzoo.org.uk/
Friends of the Earth, 26-28 Underwood Street, London N1 7JQ Tel: 020 7490 1555
http://www.foe.co.uk/
Greenpeace, Canonbury Villas, London N1 2PN Tel: 020 7865 8100
http://www.greenpeace.org.uk/
The Royal Society for the Protection of Birds (RSPB) The Lodge, Sandy, Bedfordshire, SG19 2DL Tel: 01767 680551
http://www.rspb.org.uk/
Survival International, 6 Charterhouse Buildings, London EC1M 7ET Tel: 020 7687 8700
http://www.survival-international.org/
WWF–UK, Panda House, Weyside Park, Godalming, Surrey GU7 1XR Tel: 01483 426444
http://www.wwf.org.uk/

INDEX

Picture acknowledgements:
All photographs are by Edward Parker with the exception of the following: OSF 7 (John Chellman), 9 top (Robin Bush), 13 left (Kjell Sandved), 15 (Konrad Wothe), 18 bottom (Michael Sewell), 21 top (Tui de Roy), 25 (Joe B. Blossom), 27 and *cover* (Michael Fogden), 33 top (Eric Woods), 45 top (Michael Fogden).